Sermon Outlines on the Cross

Stephen F. Olford

 **Baker Books**

A Division of Baker Book House Co
Grand Rapids, Michigan 49516

© 1997 by Stephen F. Olford
Adapted from material previously published in the Stephen Olford Biblical
Preaching Library.

Published by Baker Books
a division of Baker Book House Company
P.O. Box 6287, Grand Rapids, MI 49516-6287

Printed in the United States of America

ISBN 0-8010-9045-8

For information about academic books, resources for Christian leaders, and
all new releases available from Baker Book House, visit our web site:

http://www.bakerbooks.com

Contents

Introduction

One is a wise preacher, Bible class leader, or itinerant evangelist who takes advantage of the Christian calendar of the year for reaching the minds, hearts, and wills of his/her audience. Whether we recognize it or not, the fact remains (even in our secularized society) that people are culturally conditioned to such seasonal days as Good Friday and Easter.

In this volume we are concentrating on an important season of the year that leads up to Good Friday and Easter. We have included a series of texts that focus on Christ's work on the cross. Then we move on to an introductory message on "The Word of the Cross" and follow with a thoughtful treatment of our Savior and his suffering for us and our salvation. His seven last words are expositions that will help your listeners to feel that "they were there" when our Lord was crucified. But he rose again!—and that is why we include in this section "Journey into Joy."

As you style these outlines to your own personality as a preacher/teacher, and your own purpose as a pastor, remember what homiletical structure is all about. In the words of Ilion T. Jones: "The outlines should have unity—each point being a subthesis of the main thesis; it should have order, the points being coordinate; it should have proportion, all points being of parallel construction; it should have climax, the points being arranged in an ascending order. The wording should not be odd, smart or clever, but the points should be fresh, striking, and intriguing, without being sensational."

This is precisely what we have sought to do in these expository outlines. So "preach the word! . . . do the work of an evangelist, fulfill your ministry"—and God bless you!

Stephen F. Olford

Part One

Centrality

of the Cross

The Centrality of the Cross

1 Peter 2:13–25

Who Himself bore our sins in His own body on the tree, that we, having died to sins, might live for righteousness—by whose stripes you were healed.

1 Peter 2:24

Introduction

The cross of our Lord Jesus Christ is the outworking of God's redemptive purpose in time and in eternity. For this very reason the cross is central in God's Word as well as being central to God's world. In the Bible we find the message of the cross of Christ central in the Law, the Psalms, the Prophets, the Gospels, the Acts, the Epistles, and the Book of Revelation. To remove this recurring truth is to render the Bible meaningless. But the cross is also central to God's world. It was planted on a hill called Calvary in a land called Palestine. The cross is central in history, for the death of Christ divides human history and is the converging point of two eternities.

But, supremely, the cross of Christ is central to human experience, having an important relevance to the relationships of government and people, masters and servants, husbands and wives. A careful study of these verses makes it obvious that without submission to the Christ of the cross there can be no hope of peace, harmony, or good will. The reason for this will become clear in the passage before us. According to Peter:

I. The Cross Is God's Standard for Men (1 Peter 2:21)

A. *Absolute Sinlessness (Isaiah 53; 1 Peter 2:22)*

B. *Absolute Submissiveness (Isa. 53:7; Rom. 3:23; 1 Peter 2:23)*

II. The Cross Is God's Salvation for Men (1 Peter 2:24)

A. *Deliverance from the Penalty of Sin (1 Peter 2:24)*

B. *Deliverance from the Power of Sin (1 Peter 2:24)*

C. *Deliverance from the Poison of Sin (Isa. 53:5; 1 Peter 2:24)*

III. The Cross Is God's Satisfaction for Men (1 Peter 2:25)

A. *The Shepherd Restores the Soul (Ps. 23:1–3; Phil. 4:7; 1 Peter 1:8; 2:25; Heb. 6:19)*

B. *The Shepherd Preserves the Soul (John 10:28; 1 Thess. 5:23; 2 Tim. 1:12; 1 Peter 2:25)*

Conclusion

The Claims of the Cross

2

Matthew 27:27–32

... Him they compelled to bear His cross.

Matthew 27:32

Introduction

Once the sentence of death was pronounced, we are told that Jesus was led forth to Calvary, bearing his cross. So great was the strain and suffering of the preceding hours and so heavy was his wooden load that the Roman soldiers feared his complete collapse. We read that "... they found a man of Cyrene, Simon by name. Him they compelled to bear His cross" to Golgotha's hill (27:32). Three considerations demand our attention:

I. The Compulsion of the Cross (Matt. 27:32)

A. A Change of Direction (Matt. 27:32; Mark 15:21; Luke 9:23)

B. *A Change of Devotion (Luke 14:27; 23:26)*

II. The Costliness of the Cross (Matt. 27:32)

A. *The Shame of the Cross (John 3:19; Gal. 5:11; Heb. 12:2)*

B. *The Suffering of the Cross (Matt. 27:32; 2 Cor. 4:10–12; Phil. 3:10; Col. 1:24; 1 Peter 2:21)*

C. *The Sacrifice of the Cross (Matt. 27:32; Gal. 2:20)*

III. The Compensations of the Cross (Matt. 27:32)

A. *The Blessing of the Cross in the Home (Mark 15:21; Rom. 16:13)*

B. *The Blessing of the Cross in the Church (Acts 13:1)*

C. *The Blessing of the Cross in the World (Matt. 27:32)*

Conclusion (Luke 14:27)

The Crime of the Cross

3

Mark 15:1–15

For he [Pilate] knew that the chief priests had handed Him over because of envy.

Mark 15:10

Introduction

The sin of envy—one of the seven deadly sins mentioned in Scripture—is the outstanding crime of the cross. Envy is evil under every guise, but especially so when garbed with the vestments of pretentious piety. The fact that envy can and does penetrate the boundaries of religious life should come as a salutary warning to every heart. A threefold picture of this green-eyed monster is given us in this chapter which is sufficient to send us to the cross for deliverance. As we consider the context let us observe:

I. The Conception of the Sin of Envy (Mark 15:10)

A. *Envy Is the Rejection of the Deity of Jesus Christ (Mark 15:10; John 3:2; 11:47–53; 19:7; Rom. 1:28–29; 1 Tim. 6:3–4)*

B. *Envy Is the Rejection of the Sovereignty of Jesus Christ (Matt. 21:9, 15; Mark 15:9, 10; John 18:36–37; 19:14–15; 1 Cor. 12:3; Gal. 5:16–26; Titus 3:3; James 1:15)*

II. The Consequence of the Sin of Envy (Song of Sol. 8:6; Mark 15:10, 11)

A. *Envy Distorts the Sense of All True Value (Mark 15:11)*

B. *Envy Destroys the Source of All True Virtue (Matt. 16:16; Mark 1:24; 15:13–15; Luke 23:4)*

III. The Conquest of the Sin of Envy (Mark 15:10, 31; Luke 9:24; 23:34; John 12:24)

A. *The Saving Work of Christ (Matt. 1:21; Mark 2:7; 15:31; Luke 19:10; John 20:28; 2 Cor. 5:19, 21; 1 Tim. 1:15; Heb. 9:14)*

B. *The Saving Word of Christ (Mark 15:31; 1 Cor. 1:18; 1 Peter 1:25–2:3)*

Conclusion (1 John 1:7, 9)

The Christ of the Cross

4

Isaiah 53:1–12

> He was wounded for our transgressions, He was bruised for our iniquities; the chastisement for our peace was upon Him, and by His stripes we are healed.
>
> Isaiah 53:5

Introduction

Two Old Testament passages describe the death of Christ with remarkable comprehensiveness and arresting vividness. The first is Psalm 22, written over a thousand years before Christ; the second, Isaiah 53, penned 700 years before Jesus was born in Bethlehem. Surely, this is one of the outstanding evidences of prophetic accuracy and infallibility. For those who know their Bible, there can be no doubt that the person described in this fifty-third chapter of Isaiah is Jesus Christ. When the Ethiopian eunuch inquired of Philip the evangelist as to whom the prophet Isaiah was referring, we read that ". . . Philip opened his mouth, and beginning at this Scripture, preached Jesus to him" (Acts 8:35). So in this chapter we are confronted with the Man of Sorrows and the Christ of the cross.

Scholars point out that Isaiah 53 actually commences with the thirteenth verse of chapter 52, and that the whole section is divided into three divisions. We shall consider each in order of sequence.

I. The Majesty of the Savior's Person (Isa. 52:13, 15)

A. *The Majesty of His Sovereignty (Isa. 52:13)*

B. *The Majesty of His Agony (Isa. 52:14; Matt. 26:67–68; 27:27–30)*

C. *The Majesty of His Victory (Isa. 52:15; Phil. 2:10–11)*

II. The Mystery of the Savior's Passion (Isa. 53:1, 2–9; 1 Cor. 1:23)

A. *There Is a Mystery About the Life of Christ (Isa. 53:2–3; Matt. 3:17; John 1:11)*

B. *There Is a Mystery About the Death of Christ (Isa. 53:1, 4, 9)*

1. In the Death of Christ There Is a Cure for Human Sickness (Isa. 53:4)

2. In the Death of Christ There Is a Comfort for Human Sorrow (Isa. 53:4)

3. In the Death of Christ There Is a Cleansing of Human Sinfulness (Isa. 53:5)

4. In the Death of Christ There Is a Conquest for Human Straying (Isa. 53:6, 7, 9; Luke 19:10)

III. The Ministry of Our Savior's Purpose (Isa. 53:10, 11–12)

A. *There Is the Purpose of Spiritual Fertility (Gen. 48:11; Ps. 128:6; Isa. 53:10; Rom. 8:29; Phil. 2:12)*

B. *There Is the Purpose of Spiritual Longevity (Ps. 91:16; Prov. 3:16; Isa. 53:10; John 14:19; Rev. 1:18)*

C. *There Is the Purpose of Spiritual Prosperity (Isa. 53:10)*

D. *There Is the Purpose of Spiritual Maturity (Isa. 53:11; Eph. 4:13; Col. 1:24)*

E. *There Is the Purpose of Spiritual Activity*
   (Isa. 53:11; John 20:21–23; Heb. 7:25)

F. *There Is the Purpose of Spiritual Supremacy*
   (Isa. 53:12; 1 Cor. 1:24; Heb. 1:3)

Conclusion

The Conquest of the Cross

5

John 20:19–23

... the first day of the week, when the doors were shut ... Jesus came ... and said to them, "Peace be with you." When He had said this, He showed them His hands and His side.

John 20:19–20

Introduction

In a famous church in Copenhagen, Denmark there is a statue of our Lord showing him alive with nail-pierced hands outstretched. He is in the middle of his disciples—six on one side, six on the other; and of that number the apostle Paul takes the place of Judas. Visitors who pause to look at the statue are moved deeply because they do not see a victim— an emaciated Christ upon a cross—but rather a risen Lord, displaying the battle scars of his triumph over death, standing among his own, and commissioning them to service.

It is this kind of vision that John gives us here in this passage. When our Lord appeared to the disciples in the upper room, following his resurrection, the first thing he did was to show them his hands and side. These scars of the Savior speak of:

I. The Savior's Personal Identity (Luke 24:40; John 20:19–20)

A. *The Christ of Calvary (John 20:20; Rev. 5:6)*

B. *The Christ of Victory (Luke 24:37; John 20:19, 21, 26; Col. 1:20)*

II. The Savior's Powerful Authority (Matt. 28:18–19; Luke 2:49; John 4:34; 9:4; 19:30; 20:20–21)

A. *He Conditioned His Disciples for Service (Matt. 26:39; John 20:21)*

B. *He Commissioned His Disciples for Service (John 20:21; Acts 1:8)*

III. The Savior's Plentiful Sufficiency (John 19:34; 20:22–23)

    A. *The Sufficiency for Holy Living (John 20:22; Eph. 5:18)*

    B. *The Sufficiency for Mighty Preaching (Mark 16:15–16; John 20:23; Acts 2:36; Rom. 11:22; 1 Cor. 1:18; 2 Cor. 2:15–16)*

Conclusion

Part Two

Words from the Cross

Leading to Easter

The Word of the Cross

6

1 Corinthians 1:18–25

The word of the cross is folly to those who are perish-
ing; but to us who are being saved it is the power of God.

1 Corinthians 1:18 RSV

Introduction

The phrase that sums up Paul's concept of the gospel of
our Lord and Savior Jesus Christ is found in verse 18 of this
first chapter of 1 Corinthians. It is "the word of the cross."
The phrase is not only expressive but suggestive. There are
three aspects of the word which come to us from the cross
of Christ:

I. The Revelation of God to Men (1 Cor. 1:18, 24)

A. *The Revelation of the Power of God (1 Cor. 1:24)*

1. The Power by Which Christ Came (Luke 1:35)

2. The Power by Which Christ Lived (Rom. 1:3–4)

3. The Power by Which Christ Died (1 Cor. 1:18; 2 Cor. 5:21)

4. The Power by Which Christ Rose (Eph. 1:19–20)

5. The Power by Which Christ Saves (Rom. 1:16)

B. *The Revelation of the Wisdom of God (1 Cor. 1:24, 30)*

1. The Revelation of Christ as Our Righteousness (Job 25:4; Rom. 4:25; 1 Cor. 1:30)

2. The Revelation of Christ as Our Sanctification (1 Cor. 1:30)

3. The Revelation of Christ as Our Redemption (1 Cor. 1:21, 30)

II. The Proclamation of God to Man (1 Cor. 1:18)

A. *The Proclamation of the Cross Is Sometimes Offensive (1 Cor. 1:21, 23)*

B. *The Proclamation of the Cross Is at All Times Decisive (1 Cor. 1:18)*

C. *The Proclamation of the Cross Is Ofttimes*

   Redemptive (1 Cor. 1:24)

III. The Invitation of God to Man (1 Cor. 1:18)

A. *God's Pleasure in the Invitation of the Gospel (Gen. 3:9; 1 Cor. 1:21)*

B. *God's Purpose in the Invitation of the Gospel (1 Cor. 1:18)*

C. *God's Process in the Invitation of the Gospel (1 Cor. 1:21, 24)*

Conclusion

The Word of Forgiveness

7

Luke 23:33–38

"Father, forgive them; for they know not what they do."

Luke 23:34 KJV

Introduction

The last words of a dying friend are always impressive and memorable. Stephen Olford did not have the honor of sitting at the bedside of his father during the closing moments of his dad's life; young Stephen was away conducting an evangelistic crusade. But he was told that his father's last remarks concerning him were, "Tell the lad to preach the Word." These words meant a tremendous lot to him and may explain something of the fire and fervency that inspire his preaching.

Similarly, the words of our Lord, as he hung upon the cross, are precious indeed! We think now particularly of the word of forgiveness—"Father, forgive them; for they know not what they do" (23:34). We marvel as we think of the setting of these words. The Savior was hanging there in agony.

Spikes had been hammered through his quivering flesh; the instrument of torture had been raised and allowed to fall into its receptacle with such a jolt that all his bones were out of joint; he had been spat upon; his body had been lacerated with the Roman whips; and in such excruciating pain and agony the first words that fell from his blessed lips were those of forgiveness.

Dr. David Smith in his *Life of Christ* speaks of the kind of thing that often happened when criminals were crucified. They shrieked, yelled, cursed, and spat at their torturers. But here is one who could only say "Father, forgive them" (23:34 KJV). Here we see, first of all:

I. The Prayer of Forgiving Love (Luke 23:34)

A. *The Submissiveness of His Petition (Matt. 26:42; 27:46; Luke 23:34)*

B. *The Inclusiveness of His Intention (Luke 23:34)*

C. *The Redemptiveness of His Contention (Matt. 27:4; Luke 23:34, 41; Acts 3:17; 1 Cor. 2:8; 1 Tim. 1:13)*

II. The Power of Forgiving Love (Luke 23:34)

A. *It Is Magnetic (John 12:32)*

    B. *It Is Dynamic (Matt. 27:54; Luke 23:34, 43, 47; Acts 2:36; 1 Cor. 1:18)*

III. The Pattern of Forgiving Love (Luke 23:34)

    A. *There Is a Cross That We Must Bear (Luke 23:34; Phil. 3:10)*

    B. *There Is a Christ That We Must Share (Luke 23:34; Acts 7:60; Eph. 4:31–32)*

Conclusion (1 Peter 2:21; Rev. 5:9–10)

The Word of Assurance

8

Luke 23:39–43

"Today you will be with Me in Paradise."

Luke 23:43

Introduction

This second "word from the cross" might be called "The Response of the Savior to the Request of the Sinner," and that is how we shall think of it in our meditation now. We can never contemplate the exchanges of that dramatic dialogue without being solemnly impressed with two things: the sinfulness of man, and the sovereignty of God. To crucify the Lord Jesus was the greatest of all crimes, but to add to the shame of it the holy, sinless Son of God was crucified with thieves, brigands, and murderers.

Oh, the exceeding sinfulness and corruption of the human heart! You and I stand there. What happened at Calvary is but the outward expression of all that is inherent in our evil natures. Over against this sinfulness of man, however, is the gracious and wonderful sovereignty of God.

Have you ever pondered why God permitted his Son to be crucified between malefactors? Have you ever realized that all that happened on that fateful day was determined before to be done? Hundreds of years before, Isaiah the prophet foretold that he would be "numbered with the transgressors, . . . and made intercession for the transgressors" (Isa. 53:12). It was an act which magnified the sovereignty and grace of God. Of those two men one became penitent and was gloriously saved—that none need despair, but only one was saved—that none might presume. The impenitent one continued to sleep in his sin, and to all his other transgressions added the impudent irony of railing against the Son of God in his dying moments. One was saved, the other was lost. That is the challenge of the gospel message.

Now let us focus our attention on the dialogue between the Savior and the sinner who was saved. Look, first of all, at:

I. The Sinner's Request (Luke 23:42)

A. *A Distressing Fate (Matt. 27:44; Luke 23:32; Eph. 2:1, 12)*

B. *A Disturbing Fear (Luke 23:40)*

1. Incriminating Deeds (Luke 23:40–41; Rom. 14:12)

2. Impending Doom (Prov. 9:10; Luke 23:40; Acts 16:30; 17:31; Rom. 3:18; Heb. 9:27)

C. *A Dawning Faith (Luke 23:34, 38, 42)*

1. The Divine Savior (Luke 23:42; 1 Cor. 12:3)

2. The Divine Sovereign (Luke 23:42)

II. The Savior's Response (Luke 23:43)

A. *Immediate Salvation (Luke 23:43)*

B. *Infinite Satisfaction (Ps. 16:11; Luke 23:43)*

Conclusion

The Word of Affection

9

John 19:25–27

Jesus ... said to His mother, "Woman, behold your son!"
Then He said to the disciple, "Behold your mother!"

John 19:26–27

Introduction

This third word from the cross conjures up one of the tenderest scenes to be witnessed on that all-eventful day. Four women and one man had edged their way up Mount Calvary's slope until they were now standing beneath the center cross. They were Mary, the mother of Jesus; Mary, the wife of Cleophas; Salome, John's mother; Mary Magdalene; and the disciple John. Stunned and silenced by all that had been enacted before their eyes, they stood brokenhearted, helpless, listening. Would the Master speak again? If so, not a word must be missed. We read that "when Jesus therefore saw His mother, and the disciple whom He loved standing by, He said to His mother, 'Woman, behold your son!' Then he said to the disciple, 'Behold, your mother!'" (19:26–27).

In that word of affection the Savior lifted all human relationships out of the disharmony and sordidness, into which sin had brought them, into the purity, glory, and wonder of what they can be and mean, through the work of his cross. The relationship featured here is the filial one—the love of a son for his mother. Observe, then, in this word of affection:

I. The Son's Confidence in His Mother (Luke 2:35; John 19:26)

    A. *A Sacrificing Love (Luke 2:7)*

    B. *A Sheltering Love (Matt. 2:13)*

    C. *A Succoring Love (Luke 2:51)*

    D. *A Submitting Love (John 2:3–4)*

    E. *A Suffering Love (John 19:25, 26)*

II. The Son's Courtesy to His Mother (Exod. 20:12; John 19:26)

    A. *The Courtesy of an Approved Son (Luke 2:49–52)*

    B. *The Courtesy of an Anointed Servant (Matt. 3:17; John 2:4)*

    C. *The Courtesy of an Appointed Savior (John 19:26–27)*

III. The Son's Care of His Mother (John 19:26–27; 1 Tim. 5:4, 8)

    A. *The Selflessness of the Son's Care of His Mother (Luke 23:28, 34, 43; John 19:26)*

    B. *The Thoughtfulness of the Son's Care of His Mother (John 19:26)*

    C. *The Costliness of the Son's Care of His Mother (John 19:26)*

Conclusion

The Word of Anguish

10

Matthew 27:33–50; 2 Corinthians 5:17–21

"My God, My God, why have You forsaken Me?"

Matthew 27:46

Introduction

We stand once again at the foot of the cross. It is now mid-day. For three hours the suffering body of Jesus has been exposed to the burning rays of the sun. His tortured mind has been subjected to the taunts of a ribald crowd and the assaults of the merciless powers of evil. The divine sufferer has almost reached the point of exhaustion when a supernatural phenomenon takes place. The sun is at its zenith, yet darkness falls over the whole earth. Such a darkness could not have been due to an eclipse, for it was at the time of full moon. It is a darkness that can be felt. We can imagine people returning to the city, wailing with fright, as they beat their breasts and say to one another, "Surely the judgment of God is about to fall upon us!" Suddenly a cry is heard through that midday midnight—the cry of the Son of God—"My God, My God, why have You forsaken Me?" (Matt. 27:46).

Martin Luther once sat for hours (some believe days) without food, or even disturbing his posture, gazing at those words. Then at last he rose, with amazement written all over his face, and he cried from the depths of his soul: "God forsaken of God, who can explain that?" And he never wrote anything on that text.

So with chastened spirits and subdued hearts, let us allow these words to burn into our souls and to stir us to a new love and surrender to the one who gave himself for us. Consider, first of all, how this cry of anguish expresses:

I. The Faithfulness of the Son of God (Matt. 27:46)

A. *The Faithfulness of His Reciprocal Love (John 10:17)*

B. *The Faithfulness of His Responsive Trust (Job 13:15; Matt. 27:46)*

II. The Forsakenness of the Son of God (Ps. 22:1, 3; Matt. 26:56; 27:46; John 1:11; 7:5)

A. *The Reality of Sin (Ps. 22:1, 6; John 3:14; 2 Cor. 5:21)*

B. *The Totality of Sin (Isa. 53:6; John 1:29)*

C. *The Fatality of Sin (Ezek. 18:4; John 19:30; Rom. 6:23)*

III. The Fulfillment of the Son of God (Matt. 27:46; John 19:30; 2 Cor. 5:19, 21)

A. *Reinstated (2 Sam. 14:14; Song of Sol. 2:3; 2 Cor. 5:19)*

B. *Re-created (Rom. 8:15; 2 Cor. 5:17; 2 Peter 1:4)*

Conclusion

The Word of Agony

11

Psalm 69; John 19:28–30

Jesus . . . said, "I thirst!"

John 19:28

Introduction

Jesus has already hung some six hours on the cross. The blood vessels of his sacred body are almost dried up. A dreadful fever rages through his frame. His tongue is parched and cleaves to his jaw. His lips are swollen and burn like fire. The spiritual desolation through which he has just passed has practically exhausted any remaining strength.

"Will he ever speak again?" we ask. "Can anyone so tortured by pain formulate intelligible words?" Yes, wonder of wonders, he speaks again! "I thirst," he says. It is the word of agony, for there is scarcely a greater torment known to man than that of insatiable thirst. Travelers who have experienced it in the burning deserts of the East fill us with horror as they describe the bleeding mouths, bulging eyes, hoarse cries, and unutterable agony of the thirst of death. This was our Savior's lot when he said, "I thirst." With reverent minds and chastened spirits let us consider how this word of agony reveals:

I. The Reality of the Savior's Humanity (John 19:28)

A. *He Thirsted in Life (John 4:6–7; 1 Tim. 3:16; Heb. 2:17)*

B. *He Thirsted in Death (Isa. 63:9; Matt. 4:2; John 19:28; Heb. 4:15)*

II. The Extremity of the Savior's Humiliation (John 19:28)

A. *The Humiliation of the Creator's Thirst (John 19:28; 1 Tim. 2:5)*

B. *The Humiliation of the Redeemer's Thirst (Ps. 69:3, 18–21; Matt. 27:46; Luke 16:23–24; John 19:28; Phil. 2:8)*

III. The Avidity of the Savior's Hopefulness (John 19:28, 30)

A. *The Father's Commendation of His Redemptive Work (Matt. 3:17; John 12:28; Heb. 12:2)*

B. *The Sinner's Recognition of His Redemptive Work (John 4:7; 19:28)*

Conclusion (Ps. 37:4; Matt. 5:6)

The Word of Triumph

12

John 19:28–30

"It is finished!"

John 19:30

Introduction

The sun, which has been shrouded in darkness for three hours, shines again, as if to announce the dawn of a new day. Abraham, with all the Old Testament saints, rejoiced to see this day, and was glad (see John 8:56). And those who have lived since the cross look back to it as the most significant and important day in the history of the world.

From the moistened lips of Jesus, who has been treated to a sip of vinegar administered on hyssop, comes the *greatest* word of triumph. Matthew tells us that he cried with a loud voice (see Matt. 27:46). John records what he said—"It is finished!" (John 19:30), or more literally, "Finished," or "Accomplished." "This," says J. Oswald Sanders, "is the greatest single word ever uttered." And J. Flavel adds, "Here is a sea of matter in a drop of language." We shall spend eternity contemplating this shout of victory. Meanwhile, there are four thoughts that suggest themselves to us. In this cry of triumph we have:

I. The Word of Completion (John 19:30)

A. *The Fulfilled Word of God (Luke 24:44, 46; John 19:28, 30)*

B. *The Finished Work of God (John 4:34; 5:36; 17:4; 19:28, 30; Heb. 10:11–12)*

II. The Word of Conquest (John 19:30)

A. *Triumph over the World (John 16:33; Gal. 6:14; James 4:4; 1 John 2:16)*

B. *Triumph over the Flesh (John 19:30; Rom. 6:6; 8:3; Gal. 2:20)*

C. *Triumph over the Devil (John 12:31; 19:30; Rom. 6:14; 8:37; Col. 2:15; Heb. 2:14; James 4:7)*

III. The Word of Consecration (John 19:30; Heb. 7:28)

A. *The Perfection of the Obedience of Christ (Phil. 2:8; Heb. 5:8–9; 1 Peter 2:21)*

B. *The Perfection of the Offering of Christ (Rom. 12:1; Heb. 9:14)*

IV. The Word of Challenge (John 19:30)

A. *The Believer's Certainty in Christ (John 19:30; Rom. 3:24–25; 8:30, 32; Heb. 10:10)*

B. *The Believer's Victory in Christ (John 19:30; Rom. 8:37; 2 Cor. 2:14)*

C. *The Believer's Ministry in Christ (Matt. 16:24; John 19:30; 2 Cor. 5:15, 18, 20)*

Conclusion (2 Tim. 4:7)

The Word of Confidence

13

Luke 23:46–49

"Father, into Your hands I commend My spirit."

Luke 23:46

Introduction

We now come to the last word of the seven spoken from the cross. As we examine this final utterance we find that it is mainly concerned with the divine sonship of our Lord.

When brought before Caiaphas and asked whether he was the Christ, the Son of God, Jesus answered, "It is as you said. Nevertheless, I say to you, hereafter you will see the Son of Man sitting at the right hand of the Power, and coming on the clouds of heaven." Then the high priest tore his clothes, saying, "He has spoken blasphemy!" (Matt. 26:64–65). And when Pilate declared, "I find no fault in Him," the mob cried out, "We have a law, and according to our law He ought to die, because He made Himself the Son of God" (John 19:6–7).

So in this word from the cross we hear Jesus affirming his sonship and saying, "Father." If Jesus Christ is not the Son of

God, then there is no revelation of the love of God. Were we to read John 3:16 like this—"God so loved the world that he gave an archangel," it would have no appeal. It would be like a millionaire tossing a coin to a beggar in the street—costing him nothing. But when we read that "God so loved the world that He gave His only begotten Son" we are melted and moved.

Unless we believe in the doctrine of the divine and eternal sonship, we cannot believe in Christ's atonement for sin, for only one who is infinite can pay the ransom price for the human race. No created or finite being is equal to the total act of God's creation. He must be the uncreated one—co-equal, co-eternal with the Father. If we do not believe in the divine sonship, then we know nothing of the message of a divine saviorhood—"the Father . . . sent the Son as Savior of the world" (1 John 4:14).

So we see the significance of the words, "Father, into Your hands I commend My spirit" (Luke 23:46). His Calvary experience commenced with a prayer for others, "Father, forgive them, for they do not know what they do" (23:34). It concluded with a prayer, this time for himself—"Father, into Your hands I commend My spirit" (23:46). Here, then, is affirmed:

I. Christ's Confidence in the Security of His Sonship (Luke 2:49; 23:46)

A. *The Revelation of the Essence of Sonship (Luke 23:46)*

B. *The Restoration of the Enjoyment of Sonship (Matt. 27:46; Luke 23:46; John 1:12)*

II. Christ's Confidence in the Dependency of His Sonship (Luke 23:46)

A. *In Life He Was Completely Dependent upon His Father (Ps. 31:5; Matt. 11:25–26; Mark 7:34–37; Luke 23:46; John 5:30; 11:41–44; 14:10)*

B. *In Death He Was Completely Dependent upon His Father (Ps. 16:8–10; Luke 23:46; 1 Thess. 4:13)*

III. Christ's Confidence in the Authority of His Sonship (Luke 23:46)

A. *On Calvary's Cross Jesus Ordered Death (Luke 23:46; 24:7; John 19:30)*

B. *On Calvary's Cross Jesus Overcame Death (Ps. 16:11; Luke 23:46; John 10:17–18)*

Conclusion

Journey into Joy

14

Luke 24:13–35

Two of them were traveling that same day to a village called Emmaus, which was about seven miles from Jerusalem. . . . While they conversed and reasoned, . . . Jesus Himself drew near and went with them.

Luke 24:13, 15

Introduction

The Holy Spirit has recorded this immortal story in order to teach us many lessons; supremely, that everyone of us is on the journey of life. Matthew does not record this story, nor does Mark or John, but Luke includes it in his Gospel because there is something very human about it.

The two disciples in question (some commentators believe they were husband and wife) were not part of the apostolic band. They had turned their backs on Jerusalem, with its tragedy of the cross, and were facing the sinking sun as they walked westward to Emmaus, about seven miles away.

In this account of their journey, we see the whole purpose of God, in the glorious message of the gospel, tenderly, truthfully, and thrillingly told. Notice three things about this journey into joy:

I. The Divine Conversation (Luke 24:14–15; John 1:1, 14)

A. *He Found Sad Hearts (Luke 24:15, 17, 18, 19)*

B. *He Found Slow Hearts (Luke 24:25)*

II. The Divine Confrontation (Luke 24:26–27)

A. *Prophetic Truth (Luke 24:25–27)*

B. *Historic Truth (Luke 24:26)*

C. *Dynamic Truth (Luke 24:29, 32)*

III. The Divine Consummation (Luke 24:29–30)

A. *He Satisfied Their Hearts (Luke 24:32)*

B. *He Sanctified Their Home (Luke 24:30)*

C. *He Sealed Their Happiness (Luke 24:33–34, 36, 49)*

Conclusion

Behold Your King

15

Matthew 21:1–11

Rejoice greatly, O daughter of Zion; shout, O daughter of Jerusalem: behold, thy King cometh unto thee: he is just, and having salvation; lowly, and riding upon an ass.

Zechariah 9:9 KJV

Introduction

Without question, the message of Palm Sunday is the message of the King. When the Lord Jesus rode into Jerusalem on that first Palm Sunday he offered himself as King to the nation of Israel. But as you know, he was rejected—so much so that he sat upon that mountain, and with a loud voice cried, "O Jerusalem, Jerusalem, . . . how often would I have gathered thy children together, even as a hen gathereth her chickens under her wings, and ye would not! Behold, your house is left unto you desolate" (Matt. 23:37–38 KJV). In A.D. 70 that city was razed to the ground, thus fulfilling the prophecy of our Lord.

But more than that, he came to the temple, and he found not only those who were rejecting him, but those who were robbing him, their King. Remember how he cleansed the temple and said, "My house shall be called the house of prayer; but ye have made it a den of thieves" (Matt. 21:13 KJV)? God has called each of us to be his temple, and he will never be satisfied until he is crowned as undisputed and unrivaled King in our lives.

In considering our text in Zechariah 9:9, we recognize three aspects of our Lord's sovereign rule:

I. The Majesty of the King (Zech. 9:9)

A. *The Majesty of His Righteousness (Isa. 9:6–7; Zech. 9:9)*

B. *The Majesty of His Lowliness (Zech. 9:9; Phil. 2:5–11)*

II. The Mastery of the King (Zech. 9:9)

A. *As King He Commandeered the Colt (Matt. 21:2–3; Mark 11:3; 1 Cor. 6:19–20)*

B. *As King He Controlled the Colt (Zech. 9:9; 2 Cor. 10:5)*

III. The Ministry of the King (Zech. 9:9; Matt. 1:21; Titus 2:11)

A. *He Brings Salvation from the Penalty of Sin (Rom. 3:23; 6:23; 10:13; 1 Tim. 1:15)*

B. *He Brings Salvation from the Power of Sin (1 Cor. 1:18)*

C. *He Brings Salvation from the Presence of Sin (Rom. 13:11–14; 1 Thess. 4:16–17; Heb. 9:28)*

Conclusion

The Gospel of the Resurrection

16

1 Corinthians 15:1–20

Christ died . . . was buried, and . . . rose again the third day according to the scriptures.

1 Corinthians 15:3–4 KJV

Introduction

In John Masefield's drama *The Trial of Jesus,* there is a striking passage in which the Roman centurion in command of the soldiers at the cross comes back to Pilate to hand in his report of the day's work. After the report is given, Pilate's wife beckons to the centurion and begs him to tell how the prisoner died. When the story has been told, she suddenly asks, "Do you think he is dead?" "No, lady," answers the centurion, "I don't." "Then where is he?" To which the Roman replies, "Let loose in the world, lady, where . . . no one can stop his truth."

And so it proved, for as soon as Jesus was risen and ascended, he empowered his disciples to make known the gospel of the resurrection throughout the whole of the then-known world.

The gospel of the resurrection is an indisputable fact, an indispensable faith, and an irresistible force. Perhaps nobody sets this out as clearly as does the great apostle Paul in that classic fifteenth chapter of 1 Corinthians. To him, the resurrection of the Lord Jesus was:

I. An Indisputable Fact (1 Cor. 15:1, 3–4)

    A. *A Fact of Prophecy (Gen. 3:15; Ps. 16:10–11; Isa. 53:10–11; Acts 2:25–31; 1 Cor. 15:1, 3–4)*

    B. *A Fact of History (1 Cor. 15:3–4, 5, 7–8)*

II. An Indispensable Faith (1 Cor. 15:14, 17, 19)

    A. *Faith in the Preaching of the Christ (1 Cor. 15:14)*

    B. *Faith in the Power of the Cross (Rom. 4:25; 1 Cor. 15:17; 1 Peter 1:3)*

    C. *Faith in the Prospect of the Church (Matt. 16:18; 1 Cor. 15:19; Eph. 5:27)*

III. An Irresistible Force (1 Cor. 15:54–57)

A. *A Revealed Force (John 2:19; 10:17–18; Rom. 1:4, 1 Cor. 15:54–57)*

B. *A Released Force (Acts 1:8)*

Conclusion

Jesus Is Alive

17

2 Timothy 2:1–10

Remember that Jesus Christ of the seed of David was raised from the dead according to my gospel.

2 Timothy 2:8 KJV

Introduction

No one can read the New Testament without observing that the passion and resurrection of our Lord Jesus Christ are the cardinal doctrines of our Christian faith. In the gospels we have the redemptive event; in the Acts we have the redemptive experience, and in the epistles we have the redemptive explanation of the death and resurrection of our Lord. The apostle Paul, in particular, majors on this theme in all of his writings, and insists that it is the ground of salvation and the goal of our sanctification and service.

A perfect example of this is the passage we have before us. Paul is dictating his final letter before he faces martyrdom. As he addresses Timothy, his son in the faith, he is determined that the young man shall not falter or fail under the pressures of preaching or of persecution; so he exhorts him to "remember that Jesus Christ of the seed of David was raised from the dead according to my gospel" (2:8). In other words, come what may, Jesus is alive! That fact alone guarantees endurance now and final conquest in the hour of death.

What Paul says to Timothy is the ultimate message for you and me. For us to know that Jesus is alive is all that really matters, for in our risen Lord we find the courage to live and the comfort to die. So as we look at our text we are presented with a threefold exhortation:

I. We Are to Remember the Fact of the Resurrection (2 Tim. 2:8)

    A. *There Is the Fact of the Prophetic Evidence (Gen. 3:15; 2 Sam. 7:12–13; Pss. 16:10–11; 22; 89:28; 132:17; Isaiah 53; 1 Cor. 15:3, 4; 2 Tim. 2:8)*

    B. *There Is the Fact of the Historic Evidence (Acts 4:33; 1 Cor. 15:1–11, 20; 2 Tim. 2:8)*

    C. *There Is the Fact of the Dynamic Evidence (Acts 9:1–9; 22:6–11; 26:13–16; 1 Cor. 15:8; 2 Tim. 2:8)*

II. We Are to Consider the Force of the Resurrection (2 Tim. 2:1, 8)

    A. *As Christians, We Have the Power to Stand for Christ (Rom. 8:37; 2 Tim. 2:3–4)*

    B. *As Christians, We Have the Power to Strive for Christ (2 Tim. 2:5)*

    C. *As Christians, We Have the Power to Serve for Christ (Matt. 25:23; John 15:1–8; 2 Tim. 2:6)*

III. **We Are to Deliver the Faith of the Resurrection (2 Tim. 2:8–10)**

    A. *We Must Preach the Gospel Whatever the Cost (Luke 23:32, 39; 2 Tim. 2:9, 11–12)*

    B. *We Must Preach the Gospel Wherever the Call (Mark 16:15; 2 Tim. 2:10)*

Conclusion

Stephen F. Olford is recognized internationally as a leading expository preacher. He is the son of British missionaries to West Africa. He has pastored churches in England and the United States, including Calvary Baptist Church in New York City. His ministry has included radio and television programs as well as his Encounter Ministries and the Institute for Biblical Preaching which he founded in Memphis, Tennessee to encourage and equip pastors and laypersons from around the world to carry out the Great Commission. Dr. Olford is the author of numerous books including volumes in the *Stephen Olford Biblical Preaching Library* from which this book has been adapted.